Faculty Participation
in Academic
Decision Making

ARCHIE R. DYKES

AMERICAN COUNCIL ON E

$2.00

AMERICAN COUNCIL ON EDUCATION MONOGRAPH

Faculty Participation
in Academic
Decision Making

REPORT OF A STUDY

ARCHIE R. DYKES

AMERICAN COUNCIL ON EDUCATION
1968

Archie R. Dykes is Vice President of the University of
Tennessee and Chancellor of the University of
Tennessee at Martin. His study was made while he was
an American Council on Education academic
administration fellow in 1966-67.

© 1968 American Council on Education
1785 Massachusetts Avenue
Washington, D.C.   20036

Second Printing November 1968

Library of Congress Catalog Card Number 68-9399
Printed in the United States of America

Foreword

Conceived ideally as institutions where everybody is presumed to be engaged in the pursuit of learning, colleges and universities may be regarded as enterprises in which nobody's acquisition of knowledge diminishes anybody else's possible share. If there were no other circumstances affecting the common endeavor, then perhaps there would be no competition or conflict in academe about means and ends. Actual institutions, however, are human organizations whose members do not and cannot share equally in such matters as influence, authority, and power. Entitlement to these valued possessions is inevitably a source of dispute.

Although "Who decides what?" is a question for perennial debate in academic circles, the issues it involves are likely to become more heated during a period of rapid social change, such as colleges and universities are now undergoing. Dr. Archie Dykes' study of "Faculty Participation in Academic Decision Making" is thus a timely contribution and a needed one. He is by no means the first author in the field, but he is one of the few who have ever bothered to approach it empirically. As the informed reader is aware, most writings about academic governance are based largely upon the impressions and opinions of individual commentators. Typically, they are in essay form and rely heavily upon rhetoric rather than factual inquiry to make their points.

This monograph has the virtue of being a systematic inquiry into various aspects of faculty participation in academic decision making at a large and outstanding public university. In my judgment, it succeeds in getting at the perceived and preferred roles in decision making on the part of a representative cross section of a faculty. Since the investigatory techniques employed are quite familiar in social science, it is surprising that they have not, to the best of my knowledge, been used previously to describe and analyze these important aspects of attitudes and behavior in the campus environment.

As the Table of Contents indicates, Dr. Dykes has undertaken the task of ascertaining the faculty's conceptions of its "proper" role in decision making, its satisfactions and dissatisfactions with the perceived *status quo* in campus governance, its reasons for participating, impediments to the process, and how the process operates. His study does not touch upon every possible facet of decision making, of course, but it does, in my opinion, ask and answer some of the most significant questions about academic governance. It confirms some popular notions and refutes some others. Even though the observations are confined to a single institution, my guess would be that the findings are valid for a considerable number of American universities.

Dr. Dykes' study is not primarily hortatory in its objectives but his "Conclusions" do set forth some practical guidelines for more effective faculty participation in academic decision making. His recommendations strike me as being both sensible and useful.

The author is presently a top administrative officer in another state university, but when he undertook this inquiry, he had the advantage of being a participant-observer without being immersed personally in the role of student, professor, administrator, or trustee. He was at the time a Fellow in the American Council on Education's Academic Administration Internship Program—a position which gave him entree to the academic community and also minimized the prospect of his being identified with any particular aspect of its structure.

The author's findings should be of lively concern to all who want and need to know more about who decides what and why in an academic community. Council publication of *Faculty Participation in Academic Decision Making* is the first item in what we hope will be a series of monographs on significant issues in higher education. We expect this series to meet a need and reach an audience that cannot be satisfactorily met and reached through either journal-length articles or the more extended treatment of full-length books. We intend to publish these monographs inexpensively and distribute them widely among those persons who can benefit directly from more and better knowledge about current problems of academic structure and function.

Logan Wilson, *President*
American Council on Education

Preface

Recent developments in higher education have created perplexing dilemmas for faculty participation in the governance of the academic community. Effective faculty participation in the academic decision-making processes is essential; the complex problems confronting institutions of higher education everywhere require the best efforts of the best minds available if they are to be resolved satisfactorily. Yet, the ability of faculties to play a meaningful role in decision making is increasingly challenged as institutions grow larger and more complex and as the decision-making processes become more bureaucratized and formalized.

The organizational arrangements through which faculties have traditionally participated in decisions no longer seem to secure the desired degree of participation, and dissatisfaction with what some members of the professoriate view as their increasingly secondary role appears to be growing. The more mordant critics have become outspoken in denouncing the "bureaucratization" of today's colleges and universities, what they perceive to be "administrative arbitrariness," increasing reliance on "hierarchical" as opposed to "collegial" authority, and the supposed legerdemain whereby, it is argued, mock recognition is given to faculty participation in decisions.[1] At the same time, as W. H. Cowley has observed, many of the critics seem to have forgotten that the colleges and universities were created and exist to serve the general society, and have come to believe instead that professors are the chief parties of interest and therefore should control the institutions.[2]

The rising status of the professoriate and its increasing professionalization are altering the academician's traditional attitudes toward participation in decision making. Faculty members everywhere are pressing for the full prerogatives of their newfound professionalism, witness the emerging phenomenon of "academic negotiations," academia's genteel euphemism for collective bargaining. Yet, many academicians are reluctant to become involved in the affairs of university governance; "there are bigger fish for the academic man to fry on many campuses—research contracts, consultantships, and the other spoils of the affluent academic society."[3]

---

[1] See, for example, Robert Presthus, "University Bosses: The Executive Conquest of Academe," *The New Republic,* Vol. 152 (February 20, 1965), pp. 20–24.

[2] W. H. Cowley, "Professors, Presidents, and Trustees," *AGB Reports,* Vol. 9, No. 5 (February, 1967), pp. 14–15. (Reprint of a lecture given at the University of Arizona, 1962, in the Kennecott Lecture Series.)

[3] Francis E. Rourke and Glenn E. Brooks, *The Managerial Revolution in Higher Education* (Baltimore: The Johns Hopkins Press, 1966), p. 128.

One writer has noted, perhaps with cynicism, that the low priority assigned to involvement in the decision-making processes by today's academicians sometimes results in the administration getting "advice on curriculum, educational policy, and other vital matters from those whose chief qualification is availability rather than insight or wisdom."[4] Frederic Heimberger, in a more considered statement, put the matter thus: thus:

> On this matter and at this moment there is cause for deep concern. Perhaps because of sheer size and the diversity of specialized efforts, too many faculty members seem to be losing their feelings for the university as a whole and even for their oneness in what ought to be a proud, powerful, and responsible profession. All too often their attitude is one of live and let live, of lack of interest in what may happen elsewhere on the campus so long as personal or departmental endeavors are not directly affected.[5]

Despite such expressions of concern, little effort has been made on most campuses to study systematically faculty participation in academic decision making. The decade-old remark of one observer of the higher learning that it is time for the colleges and universities to be "subjected to the same intensive analysis and study which have been brought to bear on various forms of business and industrial enterprise"[6] remains as unfulfilled today as when it was made.

The study reported here represents one attempt to subject faculty participation in academic decision making to such investigation and analysis. The study was designed to assess attitudes and perceptions of faculty members regarding faculty participation in academic decision making. If the subtleties and complexities of such participation are to be understood, professorial attitudes about it must be known. For the faculty's actual role in decision making is determined both by external forces and restraints and by the ways in which faculty members view participation. By examining these attitudes and perceptions, we may gain some insight into the consonances and dissonances of that role.

This study was conducted by means of personal interviews with the faculty of the College of Liberal Arts and Sciences of a large Midwestern university. Interviews were held with a random sample (stratified by professorial rank) of 20 percent of the College's faculty, a total of 106 persons. Faculty members who devoted a major portion of their time to administrative duties, such as department heads, were excluded from the sample.[7]

---

[4]Robert A. Nisbet, "Conflicting Academic Loyalties," in *Improving College Teaching* (Washington: American Council on Education, 1966), p. 22.

[5]Frederic Heimberger, "The State Universities," *DAEDALUS,* Vol. 93, No. 4 (Fall, 1964), pp. 1107–1108.

[6]Logan Wilson, "A President's Perspective," *Faculty-Administration Relationships,* report of a work conference sponsored by the Commission on Instruction and Evaluation of the American Council on Education, May 7–9, 1957, p. 12.

[7]Throughout this report, the term "faculty" refers only to those in the university community who devote full time to teaching or to research or both. "Administration" refers to all administrators, including department heads, deans, and campus-wide officers.

Standard interviewing procedures were followed. An interview guide was used, appropriately adjusted and refined after pretesting. To elicit candid responses, anonymity was assured to each interviewee. During the interview sessions, respondents were asked both to reply to prepared questions and to comment freely. Efforts were made to secure decisive answers, to ask probing questions when it appeared the respondent's views had not been fully expressed, and to record fully and accurately what was said. While the time required for each interview varied considerably, the average was approximately one hour.

The faculty members interviewed were first asked what they thought their "proper" role in academic decision making should be and if they were satisfied with what they saw as their actual role. Additional questions were asked to discover why faculty members involve themselves in campus decision making, what obstacles they perceive to faculty participation, and by what means participation takes place. The findings are presented in that order in the text and tables that follow, along with many of the free comments in which the respondents expressed their attitudes and reasoning. The final portion of this report presents the author's conclusions.

Archie R. Dykes

Contents

List of Tables

The Faculty's "Proper" Role
in Decision Making

Faculty members generally have strong views about what their role in decision making should be. To assess these views in a quantifiable fashion, each faculty member interviewed for this study was first asked what the faculty's role should be in six broad areas of institutional decision making: academic affairs, personnel matters, financial affairs, capital improvements, student affairs, and public and alumni relations. Five choices were presented, representing varying degrees of influence from almost complete faculty discretion (the faculty should "always" or "almost always" determine such matters) at one extreme to no faculty involvement ("the faculty has no role") at the other. Table 1 shows the five choices and the percentage of respondents choosing each alternative for each of the six areas.

Academic Affairs

This area of decision making was defined as follows: academic affairs, especially such matters as degree requirements, curricula, student admission requirements, and academic standards. Predictably, respondents prescribed a role of overwhelming influence for the faculty in such matters; 86 percent said that decisions in this area, as a minimum, should "usually" be determined by the faculty. Free comments during the interviews accentuated this conviction.

> Usually, I'm wary of such words as "always" or "almost always," but in this case there is no room for reservation; the faculty must be in control of all academic matters.

> This is the faculty's special area of competence; faculty influence must be controlling.

All of the remaining respondents thought the proper role of the faculty in academic matters was to make recommendations to the administration, but many of them made this lesser choice on practical grounds. They felt it was unrealistic to expect professors to take time from their teaching and research for involvement in decision making, even in the area of academic affairs.

> It's heretical to suggest anything other than that the faculty should control all academic affairs, but show me many professors who are willing to give the time and effort required. The fact is we are not willing; we're too busy with our own interests, with teaching and research. The demands imposed on the professor today by his discipline leave little time for anything else.

Even those who prescribed a determining role for the faculty in academic affairs saw the exercise of faculty influence as a matter of weighing and deciding proposals and recommendations offered by the administration, i.e., in reacting, not acting. "The faculty should function as a legislative branch with the administration bringing proposals and plans to it for decisions and then carrying out the faculty's will." Or, as one professor succinctly put it, "The administration proposes; the faculty disposes." Clearly, a controlling influence in academic affairs seemed to many respondents to come as much, or more, from the faculty's veto power as from any positive action it might take.

TABLE 1. The Faculty's Proper Role in Decisions
As Indicated by Percent of Faculty Members Choosing Selected Responses

Degrees of Influence	Academic Affairs	Personnel Matters	Financial Affairs	Capital Improvements	Student Affairs	Public and Alumni Relations
I. Faculty should determine:						
Always, almost always	60	44	2	8	3	0
Usually	26	25	9	13	21	0
Total	86	69	11	21	24	0
II. Faculty should recommend to administration, but latter should decide	14	31	81	75	49	44
III. Faculty should not usually be involved	0	0	8	4	25	51
IV. Faculty has no role	0	0	0	0	2	5

Personnel Matters

Another area of decision making in which faculty might be expected to claim an influential role is personnel matters. The "Statement on Government of Colleges and Universities," recently developed by three major national organizations concerned with higher education,[8] asserts, "Faculty status and related matters are primarily a faculty responsibility; this area includes appointments, reappointments, decisions not to reappoint, promotions, the granting of tenure, and dismissal." The Statement goes on to say that the role of the faculty in such matters derives from the assumption that "scholars in a particular field or activity have the chief competence for judging the work of their colleagues" and that "determinations in these matters should first be by faculty action . . . reviewed by the chief academic officers with the concurrence of the board." The faculty's judgment should be controlling, except in "rare instances" and for "compelling reasons."

Faculty respondents were asked what they thought the faculty's role should be in faculty "personnel matters, including appointments,

[8]The American Association of University Professors, the Association of Governing Boards of Universities and Colleges, and the American Council on Education.

promotions, dismissals, and the awarding of tenure." The pattern of responses (shown in Table 1) resembled that for academic decisions, but a determining role for the faculty was less emphatically asserted.

Judging from the interviewees' free comments, this lesser role derives primarily from a belief that faculty members tend to permit friendships and personal biases to influence their decisions unduly. This concern was voiced frequently, especially among those who believed that the faculty's proper role was advisory.

> The faculty should certainly be consulted, but the final decision should rest elsewhere. Too many faculty members let their decisions about colleagues be influenced by improper considerations. Decisions about personnel should be made by the administration. Faculty members may be inclined to "scratch each other's back."

A distinction was sometimes made between decisions about appointments and other personnel decisions. Apparently, the respondents believed that they and their colleagues are more likely to be impartial and able to base their evaluation on professional competence in the case of new faculty appointments; in these decisions, a more positive role was assigned. But in promotions, the granting of tenure, and especially in dismissals, concern was frequently expressed, as one professor put it, over "the tendency of the faculty to become soft in the head." In these decisions, administrative involvement was perceived as a balancing factor and as a protection against improper influences.

Still, nearly 70 percent of the faculty members interviewed believed that faculty wishes should, as a minimum, "usually" be controlling in decisions about personnel matters. In this area of decision making, the faculty's views about its proper role appear to contradict reality as described by Caplow and McGee:

> Promotions . . . often occur over the objection of some member or members of the department. . . . There are occasional reports of promotions made over the objections of a majority of a department and sometimes without the knowledge of department members.[9]

This discrepancy between what the faculty sees as desirable and what actually happens may partially explain the widespread feeling on many campuses that faculty members are viewed by the administration as employees rather than as the independent professionals which they consider themselves to be.

Financial Affairs

Students of the higher learning have noted the impracticality of separating decisions in academic affairs and in other areas in which the desirability of faculty influence is generally acknowledged from decisions about finance, in which faculty prerogatives are less well accepted. T. R. McConnell has argued that it is impossible to divide faculty and

---

[9]Theodore Caplow and Reece J. McGee, *The Academic Marketplace* (Garden City, N.Y.: Anchor Books, Doubleday and Company, Inc., 1965), p. 164. Originally published by Basic Books, Inc., 1958.

administrative prerogatives along "educational" and "budgetary" lines as if they were unrelated; "educational planning is meaningless without budgetary implementation."[10] John Millett has asserted that some way must be found "to achieve consensus about the utilization of the financial resources of a college or university for current operating purposes."[11] Rourke and Brooks have pointed out that the budget is "both a technical instrument of management and a policy document which reflects changes taking place in the academic direction of an institution."[12] But, traditionally, financial decision making has been the clear responsibility of the administration and the board of control. The faculty's dilemma has been aptly described:

> The faculty is not responsible for assuring the continued solvency of an institution. . . . It would therefore be presumptuous to assert its right to control the disposition of funds. . . . Yet it is those decisions that may have the most significance for educational policies.[13]

Faculty members' perspectives on this vital problem were sought during the interviews. The decision area was defined as: financial affairs, including determination of financial priorities and allocation of budgetary resources. The responses are shown in Table 1.

Clearly, faculty members are reticent to assign themselves a determining role; only 11 percent of the sample felt faculty influence should be decisive in financial affairs, compared with 86 percent who felt this way about academic affairs. The connection between "educational" decisions and "financial" decisions was, at best, quite evanescent in the minds of many respondents, who repeatedly showed a strong tendency to view educational and financial affairs as two different worlds. As a result, prerogatives were assigned respectively to the faculty and the administration on the rather simplistic assumption that everything "educational" belongs to the former and everything "financial" to the latter.

> As a community of scholars, the faculty should concern itself only with scholarly matters. Financial affairs and other mundane concerns are ancillary to scholarship; let the administration do the housekeeping.

The aphorism, "the faculty educates and the administration administers," was cited frequently to justify this division of responsibilities. But other reasons were also presented for the faculty's less emphatic role, including a perceived lack of acumen in financial affairs, the faculty's limited and sometimes distorted perspective of

---

[10]T. R. McConnell, "Needed Research in College and University Organization and Administration," in Terry F. Lunsford (ed.), *The Study of Academic Administration* (Boulder, Colo.: Western Interstate Commission for Higher Education, 1963), p. 122.

[11]John D. Millet, *The Academic Community: An Essay on Organization* (New York: McGraw-Hill Book Company, Inc., 1962), p. 252.

[12]Rourke and Brooks, *op. cit.,* pp. 68 - 69.

[13]Ralph S. Brown, Jr., "Rights and Responsibilities of Faculty," *AAUP Bulletin,* Vol. 52, No. 2 (June, 1966), p. 138.

institutional-wide concerns, lack of time for involvement, and the tendency of faculty members to consider financial decisions in terms of their personal and disciplinary vested interests.

Still, the respondents did not intend to exclude faculty influence. They said repeatedly that the faculty should be consulted, that it should have effective means of expressing its views when it saw fit to do so, and that its recommendations, when offered, should be listened to attentively and considered carefully. To this extent, the respondents revealed an appreciation of the implications of financial decisions for their own scholarly and intellectual interests.

Capital Improvements

The faculty's proper role in capital improvement matters (buildings, other physical facilities, and grounds), as seen by members of the sample, does not differ greatly from its role in financial affairs and is primarily one of recommending to the administration. (See Table 1.) However, 21 percent of the respondents thought the faculty, as a minimum, should "usually" determine capital improvement decisions, while only 11 percent chose this answer for financial affairs. The difference appears to come from a particular faculty viewpoint about decisions dealing with buildings and grounds. Many respondents believed that administrators tend to overemphasize physical plant development and that, concurrently, academic buildings are sometimes assigned a low priority vis-à-vis ancillary but more noticeable facilities, such as sports arenas or other buildings likely to attract public attention. The slightly stronger role prescribed for faculty in capital improvements, compared to financial decisions, may be a reaction against what is seen as misguided administrative emphasis. Consider the following stricture:

> The faculty needs an important voice in all these matters to keep the administration from wasting money on buildings. Administrators who get frustrated in other areas turn to buildings for their monuments; they become more interested in building a huge, imposing physical plant than in improving the intellectual atmosphere.

But not all who felt the faculty should have a primary role in such decisions were motivated by a wish to check administrative self-indulgence. Many believed the faculty was uniquely qualified to make decisions about capital improvements. "The faculty is best able to judge what new facilities are needed and the order in which they should be provided; after all, the faculty lives and works in them."

Of the respondents who thought the faculty's proper role was advisory, that is, to recommend to the administration (75 percent of the sample), many cited problems of insufficient time, lack of expertise, and a perceived lack of institutional perspective for their choice. To them, faculty control was not viable. The following comment is typical.

> We have administrators for these sorts of things. The faculty can't afford to get involved too deeply, but there should be ways for faculty views to be heard. And the faculty should be in a position to step in when questionable proposals are made.

Moreover, some respondents saw a danger in faculty control, implying the faculty might be less just and equitable than the administration. "Talk about logrolling; if the faculty had the final say, the strong would get stronger and the weak would get weaker."

Student Affairs

In the last few years, colleges and universities have, more and more, turned over responsibility for student affairs to professionally trained personnel who devote full time to recreation, discipline, student government, publications, and related matters. Increasingly, these specialized officers are under administrative supervision (most are viewed as administrators themselves), although many work closely with faculty committees serving in an advisory or consultative capacity. Decisions in student affairs have become more the province of administration than of faculty.

Consonant with this trend, the respondents in this study themselves perceived student affairs as primarily within the purview of the administration. (See Table 1.) Asked what the proper role of the faculty should be in decisions dealing with "student affairs, including discipline, student government, recreation, and related matters," 27 percent of the interviewees said the faculty should "not usually" be involved or that it has "no role." These respondents often showed a thoroughgoing indifference to student affairs.

> I don't view student activities with much enthusiasm. Shouldn't the administration handle these? I much prefer not to be involved.

> These sorts of things are just a damn nuisance. A man can't involve himself in such trivia and be a scholar too. Taking care of housekeeping chores of this kind is the job of the administration. The faculty has more important things to do.

But a similar proportion of the sample, 24 percent, thought that faculty should have a strong role in student affairs. This group exhibited a strong interest in student welfare and a conviction that the faculty is uniquely qualified to determine matters concerning student life.

> The faculty understands the student. Administrators, even the Dean of Students, are too far removed from the student to know much about him. Moreover, they rarely see him in a classroom setting.

> The faculty should take a very active role in student affairs. I don't like to see these decisions left to the professionals; for one thing, the faculty is more liberal. The professionals tend to take advantage of the students, to think only of their own interests. Moreover, the things they want of the students, order, compliance, docility, are quite different from what the faculty desires.

Almost half of those interviewed believed that the faculty's proper role in student affairs was to make recommendations to the administration. This function could best be accomplished, according to many in this group, through faculty advisory or consultative committees working closely with such officers as the Dean of Students. These respondents attached considerable importance to faculty surveillance of student affairs, believing that the faculty should not hesitate to interfere when decisions were proposed or made which appeared inconsistent with the university's academic goals.

Lack of contact with the students was lamented frequently, and some respondents felt this tended to vitiate faculty effectiveness in student affairs. "Faculty members, for the most part, have withdrawn from direct contact with students except in the classroom and in the office where the student may come with some specific academic problem." Others wished for greater communication with the student personnel staff; "the student personnel workers know more about the realities of education as it appears to the student than does the faculty."

Finally, some respondents saw student affairs decisions, although seemingly remote from their scholarly concerns, as important in creating proper conditions for the intellectual development of the students. These respondents thus felt they should actively involve themselves by offering recommendations and by advising and consulting with student affairs personnel when appropriate or when warranted.

In comparison with research, teaching, and other professorial interests, however, it is clear that student affairs rank very low in the academician's system of priorities. Pressed for time and realizing their lack of specialized competence, most faculty members willingly concede to professionally trained student personnel workers the primary responsibility for such decisions.

Public and Alumni Affairs

Few matters are of greater consequence to the most dearly held values of the professoriate than a university's posture with its alumni and the public. For how a university relates itself to its alumni and the general public inevitably has implications for such important faculty concerns as academic freedom and institutional autonomy.[14]

Yet, faculty members have traditionally held themselves aloof from involvement in public and alumni affairs. Few faculty members show much interest in speaking to public or alumni groups, in seeking support for the university from alumni or others, or in helping interpret the university to the public so that improved relations may result. Generally, it is only when outside pressures are brought to bear on the faculty collectively or individually that its members manifest concern about such matters.

The members of the sample exhibited the academician's traditional indifference. (See Table 1.) Even the 44 percent who felt the faculty

---

[14]See Paul F. Lazarsfeld and Wagner Thielens, Jr., *The Academic Mind* (Glencoe, Ill.: The Free Press, 1958). Their study found their pressures and outright attacks from the larger community seriously compromised academic freedom on many campuses in the decade following the end of the Second World War.

should make recommendations to the administration showed noticeable disinterest in this area of decision making. Many said that the faculty should make recommendations only when problems arose or when the administration requested them, not as a normal procedure. These same respondents, however, frequently asserted the need for faculty surveillance.

> The last thing the faculty wants to do is mess around in public and alumni affairs. These are administrative concerns and should be handled by administrators. But the faculty has to keep its eyes open; sometimes administrators become too solicitous about public opinion.

A measure of faculty responsibility for interpreting the university to the public and for developing cooperative and friendly relations with the alumni was acknowledged by some interviewees. But this was definitely a minority view which seemed to be based, at least in part, on a recognition that public and alumni support was necessary to achieve the faculty's own objectives.

> All I want is a happy atmosphere for doing research and teaching. Sometimes it is necessary to get involved in public relations in order to maintain proper conditions for one's work.

Among the 56 percent of the respondents who felt the faculty had "no role" or "usually" should not be involved, some placed the burden of public and alumni affairs on the administration in acrimonious terms. "Let the president 'sweat' these trivia; that's what his job is anyhow." Others reflected some willingness to become involved but "only when and where absolutely necessary." The problem of insufficient time, a natural contemptuousness for anything that smacks of public relations ("the faculty should not condescend"), and a perceived lack of ability in such activities ("this is a job for professionals")—all contributed to the wish to remain aloof.

A Summarizing Coda

The respondents' views about the faculty's "proper" role in various areas of institutional decision making suggest a pattern: The further removed decisions were perceived to be from academic affairs and the educational program, the less interested the faculty was in claiming an influential role. Thus, the respondents said the faculty should have a determining role in decisions about "academic matters" (including personnel), less influence in financial matters, capital improvements, and student affairs, and little involvement in public and alumni affairs.

> Direct faculty involvement should be limited to those matters immediately related to academic affairs. Ancillary activities should be under faculty surveillance and the faculty should have the right to step in when necessary. But the faculty otherwise should not be directly involved.

> The faculty should be completely in charge of all decisions which materially affect the educational program. Beyond that, I would just as soon let the administration handle things.

But the dilemmas posed by the tendency to dichotomize decisions into educational and noneducational categories, and by the corollary tendency to depreciate the faculty's role in areas perceived as "noneducational," went largely unrecognized. Thus, faculty jurisdiction was prescribed over academic affairs and faculty personnel, while administrators were accorded control over the disposition of the financial resources upon which academic and personnel decisions ultimately depend.

The conception of the faculty as an arbiter of proposals and recommendations presented by the administration was a popular one. The following comment presents a typical view:

> The faculty ought to, in a sense, function as a legislative body with the administration in the executive role, initiating proposals and recommending courses of action and generally carrying out faculty decisions.

The attractiveness to the respondents of the legislative model, which assumes a controlling role for the faculty vis-à-vis the administration, seems to derive partly from a desire to "return" the university to a "community of scholars," with the administration relegated to an inconsequential role. Many faculty members would like to see the administration entrusted only with administering that which is dictated by the faculty. But how this might be accomplished if the administration continued to propose and initiate went unanswered, as did the question of how the efforts and energies of the faculty might be mobilized toward the definition and attainment of institutional goals.

Related to the legislative conceptualization of the faculty's role, the respondents' comments reveal, was a sense of suspicion, sometimes explicitly expressed but more frequently inferred, that decisions of considerable moment to the faculty are made from time to time without its knowledge or approval. Aggravating this feeling was a widespread conviction that faculty priorities and administrative priorities tend to be incompatible; administrators, the respondents said, are inclined to emphasize physical plant development, public relations, and other ancillary concerns over the academic program and the campus intellectual atmosphere. The respondents frequently stated a need for faculty "surveillance," faculty "checks," and faculty "veto power," even in areas where they claimed the faculty should be involved only tangentially, if at all.

If some respondents were suspicious of the administration, others sometimes doubted the justice and equity of their colleagues. A stronger role for the faculty in certain decision areas, especially financial affairs and capital improvements, was sometimes opposed because of concern that the faculty might permit personal and departmental interests to influence its choices. "If the faculty had control, vested interests would take over. The administration is usually a just arbitrator." Other respondents lamented the influence in decision making of faculty members who were not perceived as true academicians.

> I don't question the fairness of most faculty members. The trouble is that there are faculty members who are not intellectuals at all. You find some who are professors of steam plant planning. These are equated with others. They may have a Ph.D. but they still are not intellectuals. I'd just as soon have administrators making the decisions as to have them.

Some of these reservations can be traced to the tendency of many faculty members to claim comprehensive competence.

> Some academicians think that when they become faculty members they, by some kind of special grace, know everything there is to know about the higher learning. I don't put much confidence in the special grace theory. There are some things faculty members simply cannot be competent in; yet, many still act as if they are.

Some faculty members raised doubts about their colleagues' and their own willingness to assume an active role in academic decision making. And there were comments that suggested the doubts might be justified.

> I don't know what the faculty's role should be. As for myself, I like it best when left alone to do teaching and research. I just don't have time for activities not directly related to my scholarship. So long as the administrators do what I want, I'd just as soon not be involved. You could say I prefer a benevolent despotism to any other system.

> Frankly, I couldn't care less about the "faculty's proper role." I'm just not interested in this kind of thing. These sorts of concerns don't interest anybody but the campus politicians.

Finally, the responses of the sample reflected considerable ambivalence about faculty participation in general. On one hand, the respondents prescribed an active, influential role in decisions; on the other, they showed a strong reticence to give the time and energy such a role demands. Claiming the right to manage their own affairs as a society of scholars, they revealed an ubiquitous dislike for participation in faculty government; and not wishing to assume the burden of decision making themselves, they were reluctant to accord others the right to do so.

Faculty Satisfaction with Its Role in Decision Making

This portion of the study concerned the degree to which the faculty is satisfied with its actual role in academic decision making. One major determinant of satisfaction or dissatisfaction is the relationship the faculty perceives between its conception of what its role in decision making ideally *should* be and what it believes its role *is* in reality. If the faculty perceives little correlation between its idealized role and its actual role, there is a high probability of dissatisfaction. Conversely, little or no disparity between the idealized and actual roles should produce satisfaction.

Respondents were asked to choose from five possible descriptions the one that best expressed the faculty's actual role on the campus, as compared ot its "ideal" role. Table 2 shows the question asked, the five alternative descriptions, and the percentage of respondents choosing each statement. It is clear from Table 2 that a discrepancy does, in fact, exist between the respondents' conception of the faculty's ideal role in decision making and its actual role. Only 2 percent thought the actual role of the faculty matched their conception of its "ideal" role. Perhaps such a finding should be expected, given the academician's sometimes quixotic expectations about faculty involvement in decision making. But whatever the reason, there is a gap between the ideal and actual roles of the faculty, as seen by the respondents.

Comments from the respondents suggested that the discrepancy is primarily attributable to two related convictions: that the faculty's actual involvement in decision making is for the most part focused on rather insignificant matters; and that the faculty should have a larger, more active, and more influential role in the decision-making porcesses. According to respondents, the truth of their first conviction renders impossible

TABLE 2. A Question on Ideal and Actual Roles

Which of the statements below, when measured against your conception of what the faculty's role in decision making ideally should be, best expresses your personal feelings about the faculty's actual role on this campus?

	Statements	Percentage of Respondents Choosing
A.	The faculty is involved too much in decision making; considering other responsibilities there is altogether too much demand on faculty members.	2%
B.	The degree of faculty involvement and faculty influence on decisions is just about right.	2%
C.	The faculty's role is not what it should be ideally, but it is about what one can realistically expect.	44%
D.	The faculty has too little influence on decisions; more of the decision-making power should rest with the faculty.	51%
E.	Don't know or no answer.	1%

the attainment of the second. Many expressed frustration and exasperation with extensive involvement in what seemed to them relatively unimportant matters.

It's amazing how much of the faculty's time is taken in meetings approving innocuous resolutions, listening to piddling announcements, and discussing perfunctory administrative decisions that some secretary could decide. After contending with such trivia, the faculty has neither the time nor the will to do anything significant. Our energy is dissipated on matters that don't make a damn.

The interviewees also complained about time consuming committee work; the burden of keeping informed about departmental, college, and institutional affairs; the difficulty of finding time for meetings; the frustration of trying to secure agreement among strong-willed and sometimes obstreperous faculty members; the agonizingly slow workings of faculty government; and the academician's propensity for haggling over details. Most respondents recognized these as obstacles to the more active, more influential, and larger role they desired for the faculty. Few had suggestions about how to overcome these difficulties.

The faculty's unsatisfactory role in decision making was often blamed on the "administration." Judging from free comments, fully a quarter of the respondents cited "administrative aggrandizement" for what they saw as the faculty's inadequate involvement and lack of influence.

In my sixteen years here, I've witnessed a steady erosion of faculty influence in the face of relentless administrative expansion and the usurpation of prerogatives which once belonged to the faculty. The more administrators there are, the greater their influence and the more decisions they make.

Other, more cynical respondents blamed administrative machinations.

They (administrators) deliberately burden the faculty with busywork so we won't have time for more important matters.

Administrators use the old dodge of saying they always consult the faculty, but their trick is to consult after it's too late to influence. Another gimmick is to make important decisions in June when the faculty is away. August is another time to watch.

On the other hand, about an equal number of respondents suggested that conscientious efforts by various administrative officers to secure meaningful faculty participation in decision making contributed significantly to faculty satisfaction. This idea came especially from those who thought that the faculty's role, while not what it ideally should be, was about what could be expected, given existing conditions in higher education. Apparently, many of these people not only held the administration blameless for the deficiencies in the faculty's role but, in fact, believed the administration was trying to secure a more viable role in decision making for the faculty. And some respondents in this group placed the responsibility for inadequate involvement squarely on faculty members themselves.

You can't get people concerned about their responsibilities in institutional affairs. I know everybody complains about the faculty's ineffective role in decision making. But just try to get somebody to serve on a faculty committee, even an important one, and you'll find out they talk one way and act another. Everybody is too busy doing research and writing, too busy climbing the status ladder, to take the time.

Faculty Exclusion from Decisions

As universities grow larger and more complex, they tend to take on characteristics of other large organizations; structural superordination and subordination are accentuated, rules and regulations become more important, hierarchical authority increases, and universities move away from the characteristics of community and collegiality. In a word, they become bureaucratic.

One result of bureaucratization is that decisions tend increasingly to be placed in the hands of specialized experts somewhat removed from the rank and file members of the organization. As Burton Clark has noted, specialists are appointed to various areas of administration, given authority, and expected to make decisions by the rulebook. Thus, in most large organizations, a tug of war is engendered between administrators and staff professionals over who will make which decisions.[15]

For the academician in a large university, the problem is especially troublesome. Viewing himself as a highly trained specialist with a comprehensive claim to competence, he is likely to be acutely sensitive to exclusion from any decision in which he feels a legitimate right to participate, and, if he experiences repeated exclusion, is likely to be highly dissatisfied. Thus, it seemed important in this study to determine the extent to which faculty members feel excluded from decisions in which they believe they should be involved. The question asked of each person interviewed, and the responses, were:

Are there presently decisions being made on this campus from which the faculty is excluded but in which the faculty, in your opinion, should be involved?	Yes	41%
	No	12%
	Don't know	47%

In this day of the large organization, a pervasive sense of isolation from the decision-making processes seems to be one of the characteristics of the professional-in-the-organization everywhere.[16] The finding that four out of every ten respondents felt the faculty was wrongly excluded from important decisions suggests that the academician is no exception. As universities grow larger and become more bureaucratized, the locus of decision making tends to become further removed from the rank and file faculty, thus significantly reducing the faculty's "sense of access." Concomitantly, the decision-making processes themselves become more complex and time consuming, placing inordinate demands on faculty members who seek to participate. The major results are a gradual decrease in faculty participation in decision making and a growing sense of exclusion.

[15]Burton R. Clark, "Faculty Organization and Authority," in Terry F. Lunsford (ed.), *op. cit.,* pp. 44-45.

[16]See, for example, William Kornhauser, *Scientists in Industry: Conflict and Accommodation* (Berkeley: University of California Press, 1962).

Perhaps the most revealing aspect of the data shown above is not the proportion of respondents who thought the faculty was or was not excluded from decisions in which it should be involved, but rather the proportion who *did not know whether* the faculty was excluded. The most logical explanation for this high degree of uncertainty, as many respondents suggested, is the above-mentioned shift in the locus of decision making from lower to higher levels of the organizational hierarchy, which reduces the visibility of the decision-making processes. Moreover, as decisions are shifted upward, an accompanying change occurs in the pattern of decision making; one might say it moves from direct democracy to representative government. No longer can the faculty take part en masse; instead, participation must be delegated to representatives and to committees, further reducing faculty involvement and a sense of access to the decision-making processes.

As a result of these changes, rank and file faculty members have a myopic view of what decisions are made, where they are made, and who makes them. They may not be in a position to determine whether they are, in fact, excluded from decisions in which they ought to share, as the following comments indicate.

> I don't know of any specific decisions from which the faculty is excluded, but this is probably more the result of my ignorance than anything else.

> I don't know. I assume faculty opinion is sought when and where appropriate. However, I am never consulted personally and I don't feel any direct access to decisions.

> It is terribly difficult to say yes or no. The faculty generally seems further removed from decisions than in the past. I don't know who the decision makers are, except that I'm not one of them.

Such comments illustrate in highly personal terms one dysfunctional consequence of the growth in size and complexity, and the resultant bureaucratization, of institutions of higher education.[17] As colleges and universities grow, they necessarily expand their organization and add new levels to the hierarchy. As decisions are moved upward in the hierarchy, faculty ties to the decision-making processes and a sense of participation in them become more tenuous.

Moreover, the respondents felt the greatest degree of exclusion with respect to important policy decisions normally made at the highest levels of the organizational hierarchy. The following comments were typical of this view.

> A decision has been made that the university will limit enrollment on this campus to a certain number of students; at least some of the top administrators have been quoted to that effect. So far as I know, the faculty played no part in this decision; oh, perhaps in a peripheral sort of way, but not in really deciding the issue. That such a decision had been reached came as a surprise to most of us.

[17]See Rourke and Brooks, *op. cit.,* pp. 4-8.

Much has been said of late about the orientation of this campus toward graduate education in contrast to undergraduate education. If I understand correctly, undergraduate enrollment is to be sharply curtailed while graduate enrollment is to be expanded. It so happens I agree with the decision to move in this direction, but the decision to do so was not made by the faculty. Yet, it is a profoundly important educational decision.

The faculty appears to be excluded completely from decisions being reached between the university and the State Board of Higher Education. For example, it has been publicized that the university and the State Board have decided to develop two new campuses within the university system. The faculty has not been involved in any way in this decision, so far as I know.

The legitimacy of the faculty's claim to participation in decisions such as these may be questioned. The respondents, however, clearly felt that such decisions were within the purview of the faculty, and were acutely sensitive to their perceived exclusion. One comment reveals how far removed from such decisions some faculty members feel:

Just how and by whom some of the top level decisions are made is hazy to me. The faculty never knows, in some instances, whether a given decision was made by the top administrators on this campus, the Board of Trustees, the State Board of Higher Education, or by someone else. There is a chasm between those who make decisions and those who are affected by them.

Faculty Assessment of Satisfaction

Finally, each respondent was asked to make a general assessment of the faculty's satisfaction with its role in decision making. The question and the responses were:

Speaking generally, would you say the faculty is very well satisfied, satisfied, dissatisfied, or very dissatisfied with its role in decision making?	Very well satisfied 0% Satisfied 28% Dissatisfied 53% Very dissatisfied 10% Don't know 9%

Then, to determine the sources of dissatisfaction, an additional question was posed:

In your opinion, what contributes most to faculty dissatisfaction with respect to decision making on this campus?

A feeling that the faculty is not kept adequately informed and a corollary suspicion that important decisions are frequently made without faculty knowledge or consultation are the most important sources of faculty dissatisfaction. Several respondents lamented the vacuum between the faculty and top-level administrative officers and the obstacles this raised to faculty participation. Others decried the clogged lines of communication and the difficulty of trying to communicate upward. "Our department head told us to put all our correspondence to the Dean on yellow paper because he doesn't read anything else."

The respondents also noted frequently the ineffectiveness of certain formal procedures through which the administration attempts to communicate downward. "The official newsletter is filled with laudatory comments and pious platitudes no one cares about. The really interesting and relevant information comes by word of mouth from one faculty member to another."

The influence wielded by nonacademic personnel in the decision-making processes is another source of faculty discontent.

> The auxiliary people sometimes have more influence than the faculty. They aren't trained to give proper weight to faculty opinions and wishes, and their officers have far too much authority. This is a source of irritation to many faculty members. I was appalled when I first came here to be told by one of the physical plant men I couldn't drive a nail in the wall to hang a chart.

Finally, a few respondents cited administrative manipulation as a cause of dissatisfaction. In their view, such manipulation was deliberately designed to vitiate faculty influence in decisions and to enable the administration to conduct the affairs of the institution arbitrarily and by administrative fiat.

Why Do Faculty Members Participate?

In spite of obstacles and dissatisfactions, faculty members do give their time and energies to academic decision making. Accordingly, the study included a question designed to elicit views on the forces and influences which move faculty members to involve themselves. Respondents were asked to assess on a five-point scale, ranging from "very much" to "very little," the extent to which certain selected factors motivate participation. The question and the ten selected factors, arranged in rank order according to their relative importance (composite score) as motivating forces, are shown in Table 3.

Judging from the scores, the three highest-ranked factors are in a class by themselves in providing the major impetus for faculty participation in decision making. Somewhat paradoxically, the first-ranked motivational influence, a sense of personal duty, is idealistic and somewhat altruistically oriented, while the second, protection of faculty interests, suggests a self-seeking, egoistic outlook. The first apparently stems from the academician's image of himself as an independent professional serving the high ideals of faculty autonomy and freedom in teaching and scholarship through his participation. The second comes from a desire to secure personal or departmental vested interests ("nothing motivates the academician like his interest in his own bailiwick"). The third-ranked influence, desire for a voice in decisions affecting faculty, is rooted in the basic ethos of American culture.

A feeling of responsibility to the university ranked fourth as a motivational force. The importance accorded this item is somewhat surprising, in view of the surfeit of literature asserting the current orientation of the professor to scholarship and his disciplinary peers and his declining interest in and loyalty to his institution.[18] A sense of institutional responsibility is not a primary motivating force, but

TABLE 3. A Question on Faculty Motivation

Based on your personal observations, would you indicate the extent to which faculty members are motivated to participate in decision making by the reasons below?

Rank Order	Reasons Faculty Members Participate	Composite Score*
1	A sense of personal duty as a member of the academic profession.	79.2
2	It is necessary to protect their interests.	75.0
3	They want a voice in decisions which affect them.	73.0
4	A feeling of responsibility to the university.	59.6
5	They like the influence it brings.	40.3
6	It is a factor in promotions and salary increments.	36.6
7	Personal enjoyment and sense of accomplishment.	26.9
8	It is expected of the faculty.	21.1
9	It brings them recognition from the administration.	20.0
10	It gives them status with the faculty.	17.5

*Possible range, 100 to 1.

clearly it carries some weight. Moreover, as one respondent pointed out, it cannot be assumed that only the "locally" oriented faculty members are so motivated.

> You can't say the researcher or cosmopolitan professor is not affected; the professor in our department with the largest research grant is deeply interested in the university and participates in institutional affairs more than any of us.

There are some professors who regard participation as an obligation and are willing to devote time to it. But the interviews suggest that these are the older, more established members of the faculty with a relatively long identification with the university. Younger faculty members seem much less affected. A large number of respondents commented on a general decline in the faculty's interest in the university, and some asserted they could see "no sense of duty or responsibility whatsoever toward the university." On balance, the data tend to support Clark Kerr's contention

[18]See, for example, Robert A. Nisbet, "Conflicting Academic Loyalties," in *Improving College Teaching* (Washington: American Council on Education, 1966).

that faculty members' "concern with the general welfare of the university is eroded and they become tenants rather than owners" as a result of the new ecology of the multiversity.[19]

The factors ranked five through ten in Table 3 were all significantly less important in motivating faculty members to participate than the top four. However, enough respondents thought their colleagues participate because they like the influence it brings to give this item a composite score of 40.3, and some felt this was the primary influence in actuating some faculty. "Ten to twenty percent of the faculty members who participate are motivated purely by a desire for power." A number of respondents doubted that participation does, in fact, bring influence, a view based on the questionable standing accorded participation in the professorial status system.

The low influence attributed to promotions and salary increments as motivating forces results from the fact that participation in decision making and involvement in institutional affairs are relatively inefficacious means of securing advancement.

> One associate professor in our department let a book which had been accepted for publication miss the publisher's deadline while he shouldered a heavy load of committee work. When promotions were given, he was passed over because he had not published.

Many respondents pointed out that if participation really were important in promotions and salary increases, there would be much more of it. Some acknowledged, however, that there are faculty members who seek advancement through this means. "Some people, who don't measure up in teaching and scholarship, try to make themselves by being good, solid citizens of the university."

The factor of personal enjoyment and sense of accomplishment is, on balance, of only minor importance as a motive. "A true scholar detests such distractions." Some members of the professoriate enjoy participation and derive satisfaction from it, but the respondents viewed them as less able and less committed to scholarship than their colleagues and tended to refer to them in deprecatory phrases. They were identified frequently as "politicians, the type of people who go into administration."

The last three motives for participation—it is expected of the faculty, it brings recognition from the administration, and it gives status with the faculty — were of insignificant influence. One professor summarized well the prevailing view about the influence of expectations: "It doesn't make a damn what is expected; the faculty couldn't care less." Moreover, as other observers have pointed out, declining to participate may be a way for the individual faculty member to assert his power.[20]

[19]Clark Kerr, *The Uses of the University* (Cambridge, Mass.: The Harvard University Press, 1963), p. 59.

[20]Rourke and Brooks, *op. cit.*, p. 128.

Recognition from the administration was similarly dismissed as a significant motive, except for the relatively few faculty members who have administrative ambitions. Among these people, the respondents agreed, the desire for recognition has considerable influence. "The would-be administrators participate to attract attention to themselves." That such faculty members were seeking an outlet for ambitions blocked by incompetence in scholarship was implied in many comments. One respondent put it more plainly:

> There is a myth that the administrator cannot write because of the demands placed on him; therefore, he doesn't. Many people who can't meet scholarship requirements thus go into administration. Participation becomes an escape valve; if one can't write or do research, he can escape into administration by making himself available through participation in the affairs of the institution.

Finally, the wish to secure status with the faculty was viewed as having only negligible influence as a motive. Academicians do not achieve status with their peers through participation in decision making or involvement in institutional affairs, but rather through disciplinary standing, by their reputations as scholars or researchers. For this reason, there is a tendency to denigrate the efforts of those who do become involved. "At least 50 percent of the faculty look down on those who participate." As former President Dodds of Princeton has noted, the best of the faculty tend to shun involvement in institutional affairs, young professors avoid committee work in their efforts to get ahead, and participation in organizational operations is viewed as appropriate only for the mediocre.[21] A faculty committee on the campus under study wrote in a similar vein: "The younger members of the faculty who desire advancement and tenure have learned to concentrate on their personal teaching, research and writing and to eschew involvement in the corporate life of the campus." In such a milieu, participation in decision making must be activated by something other than the wish to secure status with one's colleagues.

Other Motivations

The respondents' free comments revealed other motivational forces besides those listed in Table 3. The peculiarities of the professorial personality were frequently mentioned.

> Normally, academicians are a gregarious bunch, and we like to hear ourselves talk. But while this helps us to get involved, it is a disability once we do. The impulse to isolate and synthesize interminably all matters even remotely affecting a decision makes it impossible for a faculty group to act expeditiously. But if we didn't enjoy doing this, we wouldn't get involved at all.

> There's a certain ambivalence inherent in faculty attitudes towards participation. For example, many will actively seek to participate, will get

---

[21]Harold W. Dodds, *The Academic President—Educator or Caretaker* (New York: McGraw-Hill Book Company, Inc., 1962), p. 105.

on as many committees as possible, griping all the while. Then they will pridefully lament they're on thirteen committees.

Some academicians are obsessed with a haunting sense of inferiority which they seek to compensate for by frenetic involvement in everything going on. They feel they've got to be "in" with the people running the show.

Also, faculty are subject to "gentle" pressures, which usually are directed toward a particular kind of participation—a committee assignment, preparation of a report, or another specific responsibility. The major device through which pressure is brought is the "request." "Your department head sometimes asks if you wouldn't like to serve on a certain committee. He is requesting, but he is also your superior."

The respondents frequently mentioned the motivating power of perceived threats to personal interests. For most professors, any hint that an intrusion into their personal citadel is being made or contemplated or that any prerogative may be usurped or compromised brings them to participation with a vengeance. One respondent gave a vivid example of this reaction:

Last year, about midyear, a proposal was made by the department head and some of the younger faculty to drop Old English as a requirement for all Ph.D. candidates. You should have seen the old boys drop their research and writing and come out of their cloisters. For the rest of the year, we had almost perfect attendance at departmental faculty meetings.

More positively, a commitment to change was frequently identified as a motivating force for many faculty members. Persons so motivated were described as having "strong ideas about how things should be run" and as possessing "well-defined philosophies and objectives." These faculty members "want something done and realize they must help carry the burden."

Who Participates Most and Why?

Each respondent was asked the following two questions:

Do some faculty members participate in decision making appreciably more than others?

If yes, who are they and why do you think they participate more?

In view of the sample, the answer to the first question is a resounding "yes"; 87 percent of the respondents indicated some faculty members participate appreciably more than others. And even among the 13 percent who did not answer the question affirmatively, most indicated they did not know or could not say with assurance that some participated more than others.

I just don't know about these things. I don't participate much myself and really don't know who does. It's hard to keep up with what is going on in a big university like this.

Who participates more and why seemed to be inseparable questions, since the identification of those who participate more was frequently inextricably linked with their motives for doing so. However, three discrete categories of faculty activists are identifiable: (1) Those who have a special competence in participatory activities and thus enjoy the confidence of their colleagues ("they get things done"); (2) those who are seeking advancement of their own interests; and, (3) those who have special ties with the administration.

Most frequently mentioned in the responses were those who participate more because of special competence. Since they are effective, they are sought out as participants by both their associates and the administration.

> In any organization, you have shepherds and you have sheep. Some professors know how to utilize the decision-making processes better, they have better command of rhetoric, they are better at human relations, they know how to persuade their colleagues, they are good at compromise, and they generally have the confidence of the faculty. They are the shepherds.

> They are much better at participation; they are politicians and administrators in the best sense. Because they succeed, they are called on more. Usually, they have devoted more time and attention to the problems and have solutions they want to put in effect. Sometimes they are emerging members of the professoriate concerned with the human aspects of higher education. They're sort of reformers.

The second category of activists, those who seek to advance their own interests, was also mentioned repeatedly. They were frequently perceived as attempting to compensate for incompetence in or disinterest toward their own disciplines, but not always ("some are bright and able but unscrupulous"). In any case, discreditable motives were almost always attributed to them.

> The people who participate most are the operator types; persons who like to wheel and deal. They are busy building empires rather than devoting themselves to scholarly activities.

> Many of those who participate see this as a way of getting ahead. When they find they can't make the grade in their discipline, they turn to involvement in institutional affairs as a means of salving their ego and advancing professionally.

Finally, some faculty members are more active because of special ties with the administration which result in their having more opportunities to participate.

> Professor_____was a friend of the Provost when he was head of sociology. They still have lunch together in the Union every few days. It's just natural, I guess, that the Provost asks Old Joe's opinions about matters being considered by the administration. They feel comfortable with each other, and I'm sure the Provost thinks of Joe as a loyal, reliable faculty member, a man he can trust.

While some faculty members have more opportunities to participate because of friendship or previous associations, others are sought out, the respondents thought, because they can be "used" by unscrupulous administrators.

> There is a group of malleable but not very thoughtful faculty members who are repeatedly appointed to committee posts because the administrators know they will be amenable to whatever decisions they want made. These people participate more because they are asked more; they are asked more because they are manipulable.

The Plight of the Junior Faculty

To ascertain further who participates most and why, an attempt was made to discover whether opportunities for involvement in decision making are *equally available* to all faculty members. The aim was to find out if some faculty members who wish to participate (or to do more of it) may be constrained by restrictions, manipulation, or inadequate arrangements for participation that do not affect their colleagues.

Respondents were first asked the following question and gave the following responses:

Based on your observations, would you say all members of the faculty have *equal* opportunity to participate in decision making?	Yes	10%
	No	79%
	Don't know	11%

Additional questioning revealed that it is mainly junior faculty (those holding academic appointments at ranks below the full professorship) who do not have equal opportunity; and a large majority of respondents cited the junior faculty first when identifying those who lack an equal chance. "The system works like a law firm; the younger men are analogous to the law firm clerks, but you are not a partner in the firm until you are made a full professor."

The inequity appears to result primarily from two factors: faculty government statutes, bylaws, and traditions which prohibit junior faculty membership in certain of the more important deliberative and decision-making bodies, e.g., the Faculty Senate; and the tendency to appoint full professors to important faculty committees. These two constraints withhold from junior faculty the principal means of access to the decision-making processes.

Both junior and senior faculty respondents recognized and were critical of the inequities imposed on the junior faculty. As one might expect, however, the proportion of senior faculty members who were critical (63 percent) was significantly smaller than the proportion of junior professors (86 percent). Moreover, the senior professors were more muted in their criticism and more prone to express reservations regarding greater junior faculty involvement.

> Surely the younger men ought to be involved more, but I'm not sure they should have the same standing as the senior faculty. After all, they don't have our experience and, speaking generally, our competence.

Criticisms from the junior faculty were sharp and sometimes bitter. For example:

> When it comes to deciding things here, we're second-class citizens. We're expected to do our work and stay in our places. Oh, some of us are occasionally asked to serve on committees or even once in a rare while to make a report. But we're never allowed to forget we have not "arrived," and our opinions are given little weight. Involving us at all is just a concession to keep us happy, a kind of safety valve.

The constraints imposed by faculty oligarchies seriously inhibit the freedom of faculty members to participate effectively in the decision-making processes. In some cases, coercion from such oligarchies is keenly felt.

> Your retention and promotion depend to a great extent on the full professors. The younger faculty members feel obligated to go along with whatever they want to do. You can be "blackballed" if you offend them, both in your local department and in your discipline.

As one junior professor noted, "The impression is strong that ideas and views from younger staff are neither desired nor appreciated by the power structure of the University. Thus, 'playing it safe' is the prevailing rule."

What Impedes Faculty Participation?

What other factors may inhibit participation besides faculty government rules or constraints from faculty oligarchies? What impediments may there be in the academician's own hierarchy of values or in the other, competing aspects of his responsibilities? To explore these questions, the faculty members interviewed were asked to assess on a five-point scale, ranging from "very much" to "very little," the extent to which certain selected factors adversely affect faculty participation in decision making. The question and the items, arranged in rank order according to their indicated significance (composite score) as inhibiters, are shown in Table 4.

The demands of research are in a class by themselves as inhibiters of faculty participation in decision making. In the typical academician's system of priorities, research takes precedence over all else; it is the route to professional advancement, disciplinary status, and self-esteem. Free comments repeatedly documented the preeminence of research in the professorial value system and the conviction, despite assertions to the contrary by administrative officials, that research is what really counts when the professor's work is evaluated ("it's simple; you are promoted on this campus on the basis of your research productivity"). When research activities conflict with participation in institutional affairs, as they frequently do, the greater loyalty to research is controlling.

The feeling that too much time is spent on inconsequential matters is the second major deterrent. The tendency in faculty meetings and committee sessions to belabor relatively unimportant concerns ("at our last faculty meeting, we spent an hour discussing whether a student should drop a course after six class sessions or after eight") constituted a source of frustration and discouragement to many faculty members, the

TABLE 4. A Question on Factors Which Affect Adversely
Faculty Participation in Decision Making

Speaking of faculty members generally, would you indicate the extent to which you
feel the following factors affect adversely faculty participation in decision making?

Rank Order	Inhibiting Factors	Composite Score*
1	Takes time from research.	82.7
2	Too much time is spent on inconsequential matters.	55.7
3	Indifference of faculty members.	42.3
4	Procrastination in decision making.	34.6
5	Takes time from teaching or teaching preparation.	30.8
6	Absence from campus (professional meetings, consulting, etc.).	18.3
7	Faculty ideas and opinions are not really valued.	15.4

*Possible range, 100 to 1.

respondents believed. This concentration, in turn, contributed
substantially to a widespread indifference to participation, which was
ranked third as an inhibiter of faculty involvement.

> The emphasis on trivia accentuates an already strong faculty inclination
> toward indifference. And it's easy to be indifferent in a large university.
> About the only way to overcome it is to deal with matters in which the
> faculty is really interested, matters which make a difference.

Similarly, procrastination in decision making was seen as contributing
importantly to faculty indifference, and was rated as a deterrent of some
consequence. The reasoning behind this choice was well stated in the
following comment:

> Most people, even those who feel strongly about something, are reluctant
> to become involved because of the time it takes to get something
> accomplished. Deliberations seem to drag on interminably. Since many
> feel they can't afford the time, they just don't get involved at all.

Concern for teaching or teaching preparation was not viewed as a
significant deterrent to faculty participation in decisions. The low
importance assigned this item vis-à-vis research undoubtedly derives from
the difference in status accorded the two activities. The respondents'
comments repeatedly documented the low standing of teaching in the
faculty's hierarchy of concerns.

> Very few faculty members are much concerned about teaching. Most will
> readily give up time devoted to teaching for committee work but not their
> research time.

> There really is little interest in teaching on this campus. Of course, most of
> us have to do some; but compared to research, it really isn't very
> important. The problem is that teaching is not rewarded.

Absence from campus was viewed, on balance, as only a slight inhibiter of faculty participation, but for certain faculty members, primarily scientists, it was seen as a major obstacle. "Among the 'airport' scientists, this is very important; among the humanists, no." One respondent described pointedly how this factor adversely affects participation:

> My colleague, Professor _____, bless his money-making heart, is involved extensively in consulting work. He's away about as much as he's here. Naturally, he shuns all involvement, all committee assignments, because they interfere with his consulting. Of course, it's better to have $100.00 for a day at Brookhaven [National Laboratories] than to be here for a trifling committee assignment—at least it is for him.

The idea that faculty ideas and opinions are not really valued was accorded little importance as a deterrent to faculty involvement. Most respondents felt that faculty ideas and opinions are valued, at least to the extent expected. But a few persons, apparently influenced by their own poor experiences, disagreed strongly. "The faculty group may spend hours developing a proposal or a recommendation only to have it disregarded."

How Free Is the Faculty?

The extent to which administrative control impinges on faculty freedom has drawn the attention of many students of the higher learning. Lazarsfeld and Thielens noted in *The Academic Mind* that "authority has many indirect ways to reach its goal. The subordinate believes he has to obey certain rules."[22] Logan Wilson argued that "those who dispense largesse are certain to make dependents . . . for much of the academician's immediate welfare . . . depends on . . . how he fits into the scheme of things."[23] Robert Presthus decried the "subordination of highly skilled and learned men" to administrators,[24] and George Williams, in his provocative book, claimed that "the typical professor is in continual dread of antagonizing, irritating, or disturbing 'the administration.' "[25]

In light of such observations as these, it seemed desirable to assess the degree to which the faculty feels free to differ with the administration, on the assumption that a lack of freedom, actual or perceived, is an impediment to faculty participation. Accordingly, respondents were asked the following question:

How free do you think faculty members feel to take positions on important issues which are contrary to those of the administration?	Completely free	15%
	Fairly free	52%
	Not very free	25%
	Not free at all	4%
	No answer	4%

---

[22]Lazarsfeld and Thielens, *op. cit.*, p. 253.

[23]Logan Wilson, *The Academic Man* (New York: Oxford University Press, 1942), p. 90.

[24]Robert Presthus, *The Organizational Society* (New York: Alfred A. Knopf, 1962), p. 241.

[25]George Williams, *Some of My Best Friends Are Professors* (New York: Abelard-Schuman, 1958), p. 52.

Clearly, the faculty respondents did not feel oppressed; neither did they feel as free as some might like.

The interviewees were also asked to say why they thought the faculty did or did not feel free. Those who thought the faculty feels "completely free" based their answer on an absence of observable reprisals against faculty members who had differed with the administration. "I've never seen any evidence of reprisals, not even against those who are known as administration baiters." Moreover, evidence that the administration welcomed dissenting views are frequently presented.

> One of my colleagues wrote a letter to the Provost bitterly denouncing a certain administrative policy. He was warned not to but he did anyway. The letter was well received and he was called in to talk personally with the Provost. It now looks like the policy will be changed.

Those who thought the faculty feels "fairly free," "not very free," or "not free at all" usually cited specific examples of reprisals or direct pressures, or suggested that the fear of potential sanctions imposes its own constraints.

The following comments are typical:

> Our department head once called every member of a committee into his office about a report which the committee had submitted to the faculty. They knew he was against the report but they thought he would be open-minded about it. It didn't take him long to change their minds about that. I can't help but feel the differences are still held against the committee members when decisions on promotions and salary increases are made. Fortunately, they all had tenure.

> It's not in the tradition here to dissent. Some faculty members are very suspicious of the administration; they're afraid they won't get raises or perquisites if they speak out. I have to say I feel the same way.

Faculty members without tenure felt considerably less free than those with tenure, and among those with tenure, the degree of freedom varied directly with the professor's scholarly reputation. "The nationally known people can always go elsewhere; they have more mobility and thus more security." Paradoxically, the individual professor's marketability outside his institution appears to be his main source of security within it.

Most of the pressures and constraints that faculty members feel are manifested at the departmental level. That both subtle and direct pressures are frequently brought to bear by department heads was documented repeatedly.

> I differed with the department head once and got into trouble. Now, the "boss" is always right. I found out the hard way that it's bad politics to alienate your first line boss; he can get you where it hurts.

> Oh, you're free to express your opinions and to take your stand, but you may be penalized if you do. I don't mean the President or the Provost instigates reprisal, they don't usually hear what's being said anyhow, but your department head will be listening.

> It's easy to become known as a troublemaker if you are on the wrong side too often. When this happens at the department level, you've had it; direct sanctions can be applied there.

More generally, one may conclude that for a large proportion of faculty members, real and imagined constraints on their freedom to voice their opinions and views on important issues constitute a serious impediment to participation in decision making. The difficulties inherent in securing and sustaining a high degree of participation are magnified when those who participate must wonder if their views, honestly arrived at, may bring duress and hinder their professional advancement. But the real disability is that pressure for conformity makes for less valid and less viable decisions. The following comment from one respondent identifies the pathological dimensions of the problem.

> It seems to be part of the American character to deprecate independence of thought. Thus, we feel compelled to say everything is good, everything is fine, when actually we know it is not. For example, the faculty members in our department keep telling our department head what a wonderful job he is doing and how well everything is progressing when, in fact, the department is going to pot under his leadership and we are working feverishly to get his dismissal. By necessity, almost, we all become sycophantic liars.

Institutional Impediments

There are institutional impediments, over which individual faculty members have little or no control, which militate against faculty participation in decision making. To obtain views on the extent to which certain of these impediments adversely affect faculty participation in decision making, the question shown in Table 5 was asked. Table 5 also lists the selected items in rank order (composite score) according to the degree to which they inhibit participation.

The growth in size and complexity of the university was seen by the respondents as the chief institutional impediment to faculty participation in decision making. Their comments indicate that this factor has two dimensions: faculty members feel a sense of powerlessness and frustration in the face of bigness ("the place is just too big to figure out"); and they find it difficult to develop a definite sense of belonging to and participating in the institution ("I doubt that very many faculty members feel they count for much or have much personal significance to the university"). The net result of these consequences of university growth is to discourage faculty participation. As John Millett observed, "The faculty member . . . feels trapped in an undemocratic world where his point of view has no voice."[26]

Clearly, effective faculty participation in decision making has been made more difficult by the broad changes in the character of the campus. Several respondents lamented the "growing bureaucracy" and the decline of a "sense of community." They saw the faculty becoming further removed from the "real seats of authority" and thus less able to share in and influence decisions.

[26]Millett, *op. cit.*, p. 227.

TABLE 5. A Question on Institutional Impediments

In recent years, some people have contended that such developments as those below have contributed to a decline in faculty participation in institutional affairs. Would you indicate the extent to which you think each development has affected adversely faculty participation in decision making?

Rank Order	Institutional Impediments	Composite Score*
1	Growth in size and complexity of the university.	80.8
2	Growing orientation of faculty members to their disciplines as opposed to orientation to their institution.	69.2
3	Increasing emphasis on research and graduate education.	67.3
4	Increasing numbers of administrators.	48.0
5	Increasing relations of faculty members with government agencies, industry and foundations.	30.7
6	Greater control over university affairs from outside the university.	21.1

*Possible range, 100 to 1.

The growing orientation of faculty members to their disciplines and the increasing emphasis on research and graduate education were thought to have about equal significance as impediments to faculty participation. These developments direct the faculty member's interest away from the affairs of the institution, "which he will regard as a temporary shelter where he can pursue his career as a member of his discipline."[27] Comments from two of the respondents depict this disorientation from the institution.

> The _____ Department is so concerned about research and turning out good researchers that they don't care what happens to the university so long as their personal or departmental endeavors are not affected. Their primary concern is how they stand in comparison with other _____ departments throughout the country.

> Each little research or disciplinary empire becomes a self-contained unit; what goes on elsewhere is of no concern to its staff and what they do within their little enclave is supposed to be nobody else's business. The affairs of the whole university have had to be maintained as though on sufferance.

Many respondents noted that as the faculty becomes more segmented and fractionalized, an outgrowth of disciplinary specialization, the degree of faculty involvement in decision making diminishes, and individual faculty members feel increasingly excluded from decisions which affect them.

[27]Caplow and McGee, _op. cit._, p. 71.

Increasing numbers of administrators, an impediment which was rated on balance as much less significant than the first three factors, proved to be a sensitive issue. A small but acerbic group of commentators saw the growth of administration as the major block to participation.

> This is the main evil in the whole thing. It's not only their increasing numbers but their almost complete disregard for faculty views and opinions. To them, faculty members are hired hands. Worse, there is a tendency toward exclusively administrative careers; this is an abomination. Such men are not interested in scholarship but in building monuments to themselves.

Not everyone thought the growth of administration resulted from administrators' desires to be the chief *dramatis personae.* Some respondents felt the larger role of administration had been made necessary by changes in the university itself and, in some cases, by the failure of the faculty to fulfill its obligations.

> There are more administrators because the faculty has shown itself unwilling to give necessary time and effort to some of the duties now assumed by administrators. Somebody has to perform these; if the faculty won't act, all you can do is hire another assistant dean.

Finally, faculty relations with external agencies and greater control over university affairs from outside the institution were perceived by respondents as having little adverse impact on faculty participation in decision making. Some, however, believed that the extensive involvement of faculty members in the sciences with governmental agencies and private groups constitutes an impediment to their participation. Conversely, a few respondents suggested that such involvement might enhance faculty participation by providing greater autonomy through supplementary financial support, and, moreover, that these sources of funds might be "more friendly than the trustees and the legislature," thus further contributing to faculty independence.

How Do Faculty Members Participate?

The next portion of the study focused on organizational arrangements designed to accommodate faculty participation in decision making. The objectives were (1) to determine the relative utility of various participatory devices, and (2) to ascertain how faculty members do, in fact, participate.

The faculty members interviewed were asked to assess five devices commonly utilized to secure faculty participation on a five-point scale, ranging from "very useful" to "of little or no use." The question is shown in Table 6, along with the devices ranked in order of usefulness (composite score).

TABLE 6. The Usefulness of Participatory Devices

In your opinion, how useful is each of the following in providing opportunity for meaningful faculty participation in decision making?

Rank Order	Devices in Order of Usefulness	Composite Score*
1	Departmental staff meetings	73.0
2	*Ad hoc* faculty committees	53.9
3	Standing faculty committees	51.9
4	The Faculty Senate	46.1
5	The Local Chapter of the AAUP	36.5

*Possible range, 100 to 1.

Perhaps the most significant finding is that, except for departmental staff meetings, none of the devices is rated very high in usefulness, and none is rated very low. Their scores indicate that all the devices were thought to have some value but that none, including departmental staff meetings, was found uniformly useful as an instrument of participation.

The respondents' comments suggest that departmental staff meetings are most useful in providing opportunity for participation primarily for one reason: it is there that most decisions of real consequence to the individual professor are settled. As one observer has put it, "Just as water will always find its own proper level, so will a professor find the point or points at which his participation is important to him. . . . The department is apt to be at the very center of attention of most members of the faculty."[28] The respondents, in essence, agreed. Departmental meetings, they said repeatedly, are where "the important decisions are made" and where the faculty finds out "what's really going on"; decisions made at the departmental level are "readily transferable into action."

Clearly, the effective and meaningful participation which many faculty members experience at the departmental level is a major source of satisfaction. The personal, face-to-face relationships between colleagues and between faculty members and administrators at this level, in the view of the respondents, contribute to a sense of personal involvement in decision making that is lacking at other levels of participation. In addition, the relative autonomy of the departmental unit provides a setting in which the faculty may best realize its favored conception of itself as a group of independent professionals running their affairs much as they see fit.

> The department comes nearer to being a community of scholars than anything we have today. Here we can decide what it is we want to do and go ahead with it; we can and do agree on something one day and implement it the next. And because of a considerable degree of self-determination, we can do just about what we like.

[28]David Fellman, "The Departmental Chairman," a paper presented at the 22nd National Conference on Higher Education, March 6, 1967.

There were some dissenters from this view, however. The usefulness of departmental meetings as decision-making instruments depends greatly on the department head or chairman and his attitude toward the meetings and faculty involvement in them. Some respondents complained of autocratic department heads who use the meetings to hand down edicts that they, and perhaps a few senior professors, have already decided upon. Others lamented the deterioration of the meetings, under laissez-faire leadership, into involvement in trivia which debases them as forums for deciding matters of consequence. "Our department chairman will make no move, not even to requisition office supplies, without asking the staff to vote on it."

Faculty committees were regarded as useful devices for securing faculty participation, especially in large departments and at the college and campus-wide levels where meetings of the whole faculty are impractical. Moreover, the respondents noted frequently that the really important decisions are nearly always made in committees, or at least that the relevant alternatives are defined there, with the faculty simply approving the committees' recommendations or selecting from proposed alternatives.

Many respondents, however, thought otherwise. They pointed to the propensity of committees for delay, their frequently illogical behavior, their affinity for innocuous recommendations, and, in some cases, their lack of independence from the administration or faculty oligarchies.

> *Ad hoc* committees are frequently intended to rubber stamp decisions the "powers" want. If it is discovered a committee is going to make its own decisions, it may be disbanded. I was on a committee once which showed some sign of rebellion, and we simply quit meeting. Somebody got to the chairman.

The Faculty Senate labors under a severe disability in its capacity to provide opportunities for participation because of the exclusion of junior faculty members. In addition, its efficacy as a deliberative and decision-making body was frequently questioned ("it gets bogged down in too much that is unimportant"), and its proceedings were not a matter of widespread interest. For example, only 15 percent of the respondents who were eligible to participate in its affairs said that, in fact, they regularly did so. But some respondents perceived the Senate as a significant force in important campus-wide issues, especially when the faculty is aroused. A few thought its most important function was to "constrain an ambitious administration" and pointed out that it could, if necessary, "even rebuke the President."

Ranked last among the devices, the local chapter of the American Association of University Professors was nonetheless granted some usefulness, especially in decisions having to do with faculty remuneration, personnel matters, and academic freedom issues. Many faculty respondents perceived the AAUP not as a device to be used under normal circumstances but as a court of last resort. "It is a good safety valve; a place to go when all else fails."

Faculty attitudes toward the AAUP, as reflected by the respondents, are curiously ambivalent. Many in the sample viewed its work with favor but did not belong (56 percent were not members); others objected to it because "it is a union," but applauded its ability to bring pressure on the administration. And a few who were confronted with the abbreviation AAUP on the interview guide inquired what the letters stood for.

Finally, there were some respondents who thought that, at present, means simply are not available for the faculty to secure effective participation in decision making. These persons tended to view the university as a monolithic organization with a unitary power structure and thus beyond the influence of the rank and file faculty member. "I find all of these, the Faculty Senate, the AAUP, the department, the committees, sort of hopeless. The same clique that runs the university, runs the department, runs the AAUP, runs the Senate, and so on."

The Committee System

In the large university, much faculty decision-making power must be delegated to committees appointed both by the administration and by the faculty itself. Since such committees become the faculty's representatives in decisions, their effectiveness, in sum, determines the effectiveness of the faculty.

Because of the importance of the committee system and its presumed influence, an effort was made to determine faculty members' attitudes towards committees through the question shown in Table 7. This table lists nine statements describing faculty committees and the percentage of respondents agreeing with each description.

Item E in Table 7, the statement that committee members "always seem to come" from a relatively small group of people, deserves special attention. It earned by far the highest "score," with two-thirds of the respondents indicating agreement. Committee membership must indeed be drawn from a small pool of faculty members.[29] The respondents attributed this to a diversity of causes, ranging from manipulation of appointments by the administration to the unwillingness of most faculty members to serve. Careful analysis of the responses, however, indicates that the domination of committee membership by a small faculty group is mainly attributable to two factors: the presence of faculty members who, for various reasons, actively seek service; and the control of appointments by the Committee on Committees, an arrangement which, intentionally or not, results in a small number of faculty members being selected repeatedly for committee service.

[29]Studies on other campuses have shown similar findings. For example, Ruth Eckert found that over a period of 13 years more than 80 percent of the eligible faculty members at the University of Minnesota had held no committee appointments. (Reported by T. R. McConnell, "Needed Research in College and University Organization and Administration," in Terry F. Lunsford (ed.), op. cit., p. 119.)

TABLE 7. A Question on Faculty Committees

In a university of this size, much faculty participation in decision making must be accomplished through faculty committees. Would you give some indication of your feelings about these committees by checking the statements below with which you agree?

Statements Describing Faculty Committees	Percent of Respondents Who Agree
A.	They generally are quite representative of the faculty.	40%
B.	They are more conservative than the faculty generally.	21%
C.	They are more liberal than the faculty generally.	15%
D.	They are closer to the administration than to the faculty.	17%
E.	Their membership always seems to come from a relatively small group of faculty members.	66%
F.	The more able members of the faculty tend to be on them.	31%
G.	The campus "politicians" tend to be on them.	46%
H.	They have considerable influence on decisions.	54%
I.	They have little influence on decisions.	10%

Some observers have noted that as institutions grow larger, faculty groups tend to become bureaucratized, to take on some of the features they condemn in the administration. One aspect of such bureaucratization is the development of a faculty oligarchy or oligarchies.

The implications of such a phenomenon for faculty participation in decision making are clear. As T. R. McConnell has observed, "It is easy for [such] a small group to . . . dominate the organizational structure and to maintain control over faculty government and the decision-making processes."[30] The following interview comments are relevant:

It's nice to think . . . that every faculty member can participate in the making of decisions if he wishes. But in practice, decision-making power is in the hands of committees, and the Committee on Committees is at the apex of the power structure because it recommends all other committees. . . . It can control the decisions. There is little the individual faculty member can do to challenge the system.

A small clique controls practically all committee appointments here. If you happen not to be one of the "ins," you don't get appointed to the committees and don't have an opportunity to participate in the decisions. It's that simple.

The administration was credited by some respondents with deliberately creating inequities in faculty representation on committees.

[30] Ibid.

> All the important committees around here come from the same small group of people. They serve over and over while others don't serve at all. These are the same people the administrators call when they want to consult with the faculty. Those who happen not to be susceptible to administrative manipulation or who are not considered "safe" just don't get involved.

Others who believed the administration relies too heavily on a small group of faculty members for committee service attributed no ulterior motive to the administration. Rather, they blamed the unwillingness of many faculty members to accept committee assignments and the fact that a few faculty members had demonstrated superior competence in this type of service.

There is little feeling that the small group of perennial committee members is unrepresentative of the faculty. Forty percent of the respondents thought that committees are generally representative, while there was much less agreement that committees tend to be either more liberal or more conservative than faculty generally, or closer to the administration than to the faculty. However, 46 percent of the interviewees believed that campus "politicians" tend to be on committees, while only 31 percent thought the more able members of the faculty are usually on them. A distinction was frequently made between the types of committees on which the two types of persons tend to serve; the more able faculty usually serve on the important, prestigious committees, as the respondents saw it, while the "politicians" are relegated to the minor.

Finally, committees have considerable influence on decisions, according to 54 percent of the respondents, while only 10 percent took the opposite view. These responses confirm what was indicated repeatedly in free comments: faculty committees do wield major influence in decisions.

To Whom Do Faculty Members Go?

In determining how faculty members participate, it seemed necessary to ascertain to whom individual faculty members go about decisions at the various levels of the university's formal organizational structure. Table 8 shows the question, alternative answers, and the percentage of respondents choosing each answer.

These data show clearly that, regardless of the locus of a given decision in the organizational hierarchy, the department head is the individual faculty member's major means of access to it. "The department head is the key person; he has to be involved sooner or later and it's just good business to go to him first."

When asked why they would go to the officers they had named, the respondents overwhelmingly cited the demands of protocol. "You've got to go through appropriate channels; every faculty member knows you are to go to the department head first." But most also indicated that this is

TABLE 8. A Question on Where Faculty Members Go
to Influence Decisions

To whom would you go in an effort to influence a decision about which you felt very
strongly?

Levels of Decision Making	Officer in Central Administration	College Dean	Department Head	Influential Professor
At the departmental level?	0%	6%	86%	8%
At the college level?	3%	20%	73%	4%
At the campus-wide level?	11%	18%	68%	3%

the best way for faculty members to make their influence felt. "My
department head has influence I don't have with faculty committees and
administrators."

While protocol and effectiveness determined the choices of a majority
of the respondents, the comments of others revealed that coercion is also
a factor in directing faculty members towards use of established channels.

> The faculty is regulated in this. We are expected to go through channels.
> There are times I would prefer to go to the Dean, but I don't dare; the
> department head wouldn't like it. It's just like the army, from platoon
> sergeant to lieutenant, from lieutenant to captain. I can't conceive of
> jumping over. We have a chap who fires off nasty letters to the Dean then
> gives the department head a copy as an afterthought. He's just hanging
> himself.

If a department head is incompetent or inaccessible, the constraints
described above make circumventing him more difficult. A former
university president discussed this problem as follows:

> One matter troubled me and still does, and that was how to make each
> member of a department feel free to come to see me if and when he
> desired. Theoretically the approach was through the department head and
> the dean. Occasionally it was desirable for members of a department to
> come to me, but it was difficult to use the information they brought
> without hurting them with the department head and the dean.[31]

Influential members of the professoriate do not feel the same
compulsion to follow channels as the rank and file. "Professors of stature
feel free to break official channels. They don't hesitate to go to an
influential administrator, such as the Provost." The comment of one
respondent is especially revealing on this point: "On something I felt
strongly about, I'd probably go directly to the President by now (I'm a
senior faculty man), but a few years ago I would have said a lower level
administrator."

---

[31]Frank L. McVey and Raymond M. Hughes, *Problems of College and University
Administration* (Ames, Iowa: The Iowa State College Press, 1952), p. 152.

What is believed to be the inaccessibility of other administrators ("it's terribly difficult to reach the Dean or other administrators for an individual discussion") also forces many faculty members to rely exclusively on their department heads in most matters of concern. In fact, some of the younger faculty members do not feel they have ready access even to the departmental head, and, therefore, must enlist the aid of senior professors if their views are to be heard. These younger men accounted for the preponderance of those who indicated they would go to influential professors in an effort to influence decisions. "I would go to some senior professor because I'm young; I hardly know the department head."

Respondents who said they would go to the college dean or an officer in central administration about decisions at the college or campus-wide levels made this choice because of personal acquaintance, by virtue of their professional stature, or because they feel the requirements of protocol made such recourse permissible on decisions at these levels. Very few indicated a willingness to transgress established channels, and, for most faculty members, these begin with the department head.

Informal Participation

In addition to formal and official arrangements for participation, all organizations are characterized by informal, extralegal systems through which their membership may participate in the affairs of the organization.[32] Since these informal arrangements sometimes have significant influence on official decisions, an attempt was made to assess the importance of some of the more common ones on the campus under study. The faculty respondents were asked to indicate on a five-point scale, ranging from "very much" to "very little," the extent to which informal groups at the department, college, or campus-wide level provide opportunity for the faculty to influence decisions. The question and the responses (composite scores) to it are shown in Table 9.

Table 9.   A Question on Informal Associations

What about informal faculty associations, such as coffee groups, recreational teams, social gatherings, etc.; to what extent do you think they provide opportunity for the faculty to influence official decisions?

Levels of Decision Making	Composite Score*
A. At the departmental level	44.2
B. At the college level	21.2
C. At the campus-wide level	15.4

*Possible range, 100 to 1.

[32]See, for example, Peter M. Blau and W. Richard Scott, *Formal Organizations* (San Francisco: Chandler Publishing Company, 1962).

Only at the departmental level are informal associations seen as providing important opportunity for faculty members to influence official decisions. And even here, informal associations suffer from the disabilities of bigness and lack of personal ties among the staff. Thus, the result is the same for informal associations as for formal arrangements for participation: a relatively small number of faculty members engage in them. "Some of the senior professors who have lunch together frequently always present a united front in departmental meetings; the younger men suspect there is a syndicate." The larger the respondent's department, the more likely he was to suggest oligarchical control. The smaller departments, generally, did not seem to suffer from this disability. "We're a very informal group, just about everybody meets in the coffee room every morning. More things are settled there than anywhere else."

Although many respondents emphasized the lack of wide faculty participation in decisions through informal associations, a considerable number believed that such associations are influential at the departmental level. "The real decisions are made informally; the formal processes usually do nothing more than confirm what has been decided informally."

The respondents generally thought that the effectiveness of informal associations diminished as the locus of decisions moved upward in the organizational hierarchy. At the college and campus-wide levels, coffee groups and social gatherings accorded only minor importance in providing opportunity for faculty influence. A number of respondents, however, claimed that informal associations continued to be important beyond the departmental level; the fault, they thought, was that rank and file faculty members were largely excluded from these groups. Moreover, it was frequently suggested that top-level decisions, unlike those in the department, are so far removed from the average faculty member that he has no real insight into how they are reached. Thus, he would tend to underestimate the importance of some subtle influences. Persons who felt this way were inclined to attribute considerable importance to informal associations as instruments for faculty influence at all levels of the hierarchy; such associations were simply much less visible at the college and campus-wide levels than in the department.

Conclusions

In the body of this report, each aspect of faculty participation that was investigated—how academicians participate, what impels them to do so, what inhibits them, what their proper role should be and whether they are satisfied with it—has been reported and discussed separately. But, as the comments to the interviewer often showed, these questions were closely interrelated in the minds of the respondents. Drawing upon the study results as a whole, it is possible to frame some general conclusions about faculty attitudes toward, and perceptions of, faculty participation in academic decision making.

1. One of the most noticeable and best documented findings of the investigation is the existence of a pervasive ambivalence in faculty attitudes toward participation in decision making. The faculty members interviewed overwhelmingly indicated the faculty should have a strong, active, and influential role in decisions, especially in those areas directly related to the educational function of the university. At the same time, the respondents revealed a strong reticence to give the time such a role would require. Asserting that faculty participation is essential, they placed participation at the bottom of their professional priority list and deprecated their colleagues who do participate. Reluctant to assume the burden of guiding institutional affairs, they seemed unwilling to accord others the responsibility for doing so. And while quick to assert their right to participate, they recognized less quickly the duties participation entails.

Clearly, faculties cannot have it both ways. If they wish the strong, active role in decision making which they claim as a prerogative, they must be willing to give the time such a role demands. If they value their influence in institutional affairs, they must be willing to give such activity a higher priority among their interests and concerns. And, finally, if they are unwilling to assume the burden of participation, they must recognize that control over academic affairs will shift into the hands of others.

As Robert MacIver has noted, "An institution cannot be well governed unless each of its components clearly recognizes its obligations as well as its rights in the promotion of the common end."[33] As long as faculty members themselves are unsure about accepting the responsibilities and duties that involvement in decision making entails, their influence will inevitably diminish, not because of administrative aggrandizement or the changing circumstances of higher education, but as a result of faculty default.

2. A reluctance to recognize or accept the new realities of participation was documented repeatedly throughout the study. Nostalgia for the town meeting type of university government, for the simple devices of direct democracy, profoundly influences faculty attitudes toward participation. When colleges and universities were small, internal complexity was nonexistent, and teaching and research were carried on under relatively simple conditions, direct democracy provided adequate accommodation for faculty participation in university government. But now that colleges and universities have grown larger and more complex and the character of the campus has changed, direct democracy is no longer a viable concept.

---

[33]Robert M. MacIver, *Academic Freedom in Our Time* (New York: Columbia University Press, 1955), p. 73.

If the ideal of the always-watchful, perpetually vocal faculty, deeply involved with every issue to be decided, became a reality in today's large university, the result would be chaos. Each faculty member would have to shoulder the intolerable burden of keeping fully informed about and active in all issues while, at the same time, managing his scholarly and disciplinary obligations. Moreover, direct participation by such large numbers would paralyze the governmental machinery. There must be a division of labor in the governance of today's large, complex university; the bulk of the professoriate can and probably should be only intermittently active in decision making. In short, it is necessary to move from town hall to representative government. But the necessity for such a shift in governing style is not generally recognized or viewed with favor by faculty members. Rather, they tend to see any diminution in *direct* participation as threatening their prerogatives and influence.

In the long run, such a posture is in itself a serious threat to faculty influence. In view of the great changes occurring within today's colleges and universities, faculties cannot continue to be influential in campus decision-making processes without developing more effective arrangements for their participation. The devices of direct democracy are now cumbersome and impractical, and faculties must increasingly turn to representative techniques if they are to speak with an effective voice. As other observers have noted, "If a faculty is to be influential . . . it must be able to decide as well as to deliberate. And faculties today are not as well organized for decision and action as they are for deliberation."[34] The quixotic perception of university government as pure democracy, manifested by many faculty members, can only delay the necessary changes.

Moreover, the faculty members interviewed for this study tended to measure the present circumstances of academic government against a historical base of doubtful validity. Implicit and sometimes explicit in the comments of many respondents was an assumption that in the past, faculties have had much greater influence in and control over institutional affairs than they have now. The weight of evidence suggests, however, that this is a misreading of history. In earlier days colleges and universities were governed quite autocratically; hierarchical, as opposed to collegial, authority was supreme; the temper of the times lent legitimacy to authoritarianism; and while personal contacts between administrators and faculty were undoubtedly more numerous, there is no evidence that the closer relationship enhanced the faculty's influence. Lord Bryce spoke of the almost monarchical position of the college president towards the professors and students in the early years of this century.[35] And when a faculty member at Harvard asked President Eliot why the faculty had to

[34]Rourke and Brooks, *op. cit.,* p. 129.

[35]James Bryce, *The American Commonwealth* (New York: The Macmillan Company, 1913), p. 718.

accept so many changes, he could answer simply, "There is a new president."[36]

Many faculty members measure their role in decision making today against a romanticized perception of the past. In such a comparison, present circumstances are inevitably found wanting.

3. Respondents to the study showed a strong tendency to dichotomize decisions into "educational" and "noneducational" categories and to ascribe degrees of faculty influence accordingly. Thus, they said that faculty influence should be controlling in academic affairs (educational decisions), but that faculty should have little involvement in public and alumni affairs (noneducational decisions). In reality, such a dichotomy is arbitrary and impractical, and this kind of thinking overlooks the interrelatedness of decision areas. Decisions about student affairs, for example, an area in which the respondents assigned a secondary role to faculty, may in cumulative effect alter radically the intellectual climate of the campus and thus overshadow decisions of a more obviously academic nature.

It is impossible to separate decisions into simplistic categories like "educational" and "noneducational." If the faculty's influence is to be truly effective, surely it must be manifested in all areas, for supposedly "noneducational" decisions may have critical educational consequences. But the prevailing view of the faculty's role in decision making militates against a broader sort of participation.

4. The study findings suggest that the source of much of the tension between faculty and administration is a conviction held by many faculty members that any increase in administrative power and influence must necessarily result in a decrease in their own.[37] This view assumes that the university is a closed system with a finite power potential. The administration and the faculty are seen as adversaries competing for a limited quantity of influence. Any power or influence which the administration secures must inevitably reduce the influence of the faculty, and vice versa.

Such a perception is both invalid and seriously misleading. Given the nature of the large university today, it is possible for administrative and faculty power to increase simultaneously. Any increase in administrative power which improves the efficiency and effectiveness of the total organization potentially increases the power of the faculty, since the total power is increased. For example, a weak administration, easily manipulable by forces from outside the university, jeopardizes the faculty's autonomy and reduces its power. In such a case, increases in

[36]Frederick Rudolph, *The American College and University* (New York: Alfred A. Knopf, 1962), p. 291.

[37]It should be pointed out that many administrators similarly believe that an increase in faculty influence reduces their influence.

administrative strength obviously enhance faculty influence. Similarly, the centralization of certain business and ancillary functions may strengthen the administration, but, at the same time, may enable the faculty to exercise greater control by effectively influencing the policies governing the operation of such functions.

New perspectives about administrative/faculty relationships, therefore, seem long overdue. A clear dichotomy between administrative power and faculty power does not exist, as attractive as that idea may be in its simplicity. Rather, faculty power and administrative power are, in a sense, fused, and each depends in considerable measure on the other. So long as the faculty views the administration as its natural adversary competing for a limited amount of power and influence, and vice versa, neither the faculty nor the administration will have the strength its responsibilities warrant. The most unfortunate consequence of such a circumstance is that it forestalls effective educational leadership.

5.   The study revealed a disturbing discrepancy between what the faculty perceived its role in decision making to be on the campus under study and what its role is in reality. During the interviews, faculty members repeatedly lamented the lack of faculty involvement in decisions of considerable moment when, in fact, the faculty had been intimately involved; the administration was often criticized for failing to consult with the faculty when, in fact, the faculty had been consulted; and criticisms were often voiced that decisions had not been taken through proper channels when both protocol and university statutes had been followed scrupulously. In short, serious misconceptions existed about the processes through which decisions are made and about the role of the faculty in them. The major result was a widespread sense of suspicion and distrust.

Much of the problem is attributable to the size and complexity of the university, but they are not the only disabilities. Clearly, there is a serious communications deficiency, accentuated by the nature of the campus, not only between the faculty and the administration but among faculty members themselves.

Responsibility for the deficiency must be placed on both the administration and the faculty. Administrators—who have better access to information concerning institutional decisions—must assume the initiative in making information available to the faculty. Moreover, administrators, from the campus-wide officers to the department heads, largely control the formal systems of communication. If these are not functioning properly, they must take a larger measure of the blame. But faculty members themselves cannot be absolved of some responsibility for the communications gap. Members of the study sample exhibited a pervasive indifference to faculty government. Many proudly recounted how long it had been since they had attended a meeting of the faculty at any level, and prolonged absence from faculty meetings was for some a mark of distinction. Yet, all of them decried their lack of information and were quick to criticize the administration for its "subterfuge."

Regardless of where the blame rests, the consequences of such communications problems are indeed profound; as Chester Barnard has written, coordination and collaboration in any human enterprise is possible only when communication is effective.[38]

6. Finally, the study revealed that academicians hold an exceedingly simplistic view of the distribution of influence and power in their own community. The faculty members interviewed attributed to the administration vastly more power than it actually possesses. The constraints imposed on the administration from within and without the university were only dimly perceived, and the potency of countervailing forces was vastly underestimated. The faculty's perception of administrative power is not unlike that described by John Gardner in the 1965 *Annual Report* of the Carnegie Corporation.

> The popular notion of top leadership is a fantasy of capricious power; the top man presses a button and something remarkable happens; he gives an order as the whim strikes him, and it is obeyed.

Such a perception not only strays from reality but also hinders the development of proper relationships between administrators and faculty members. Actually, as Gardner noted, the capricious use of power is rare today in any setting; "Leaders are hedged around by constraints—tradition, constitutional limitations, the realities of the external situation, the rights and privileges of followers, and . . . the inexorable demands of large-scale organization, which does not operate on capriciousness."

Authority relationships between administration and faculty are frequently a source of stress in institutions of higher education. It seems reasonable to suppose that the relationships could be made easier if faculty perceptions of administrative power and influence were more in keeping with reality. But the process of accommodation between faculty prerogatives and administrative authority is not the basic problem. The fundamental problem is that the misunderstanding of administrative authority and the consequent separation of powers forestalls effective leadership. Without strong central leadership, the mobilization of the collective efforts of faculty and administration toward the definition and attainment of institutional goals is impossible. And without this unvarying effort toward unification, a university falls into aimlessness, drift, disunity, and disarray. It becomes something other than a *uni*versity.

---

[38]Chester I. Barnard, *The Functions of the Executive* (Cambridge, Mass.: The Harvard University Press, 1938), p. 91.

Bibliography

Barnard, Chester I. *The Functions of the Executive.* Cambridge, Mass.: The Harvard University Press, 1938.

Blau, Peter M., and W. Richard Scott. *Formal Organizations.* San Francisco: Chandler Publishing Company, 1962.

Brown, Ralph S., Jr. "Rights and Responsibilities of Faculty," *AAUP Bulletin,* Vol. 52, No. 2 (June, 1966).

Bryce, James. *The American Commonwealth.* New York: The Macmillan Company, 1913.

Caplow, Theodore, and Reece J. McGee. *The Academic Marketplace.* Garden City, N.Y.: Anchor Books, Doubleday and Company, Inc., 1965. Originally published by Basic Books, Inc., 1958.

Cowley, W. H. "Professors, Presidents, and Trustees," *AGB Reports,* Vol. 9, No. 5 (February, 1967).

Dodds, Harold W. *The Academic President — Educator or Caretaker.* New York: McGraw-Hill Book Company, Inc., 1962.

Faculty-Administration Relationships. Washington: American Council on Education. Report of a work conference sponsored by the Commission on Instruction and Evaluation of the American Council on Education, May 7-9, 1957.

Fellman, David. "The Departmental Chairman." Paper presented at the 22nd National Conference on Higher Education, March 6, 1967.

Heimberger, Frederic. "The State Universities," *DAEDALUS,* Vol. 93, No. 4 (Fall, 1964).

Improving College Teaching. Washington: American Council on Education, 1966.

Kerr, Clark. *The Uses of the University.* Cambridge, Mass.: The Harvard University Press, 1963.

Kornhauser, William. *Scientists in Industry: Conflict and Accommodation.* Berkeley: University of California Press, 1962.

Lazarsfeld, Paul F., and Wagner Thielens, Jr. *The Academic Mind.* Glencoe, Ill.: The Free Press, 1958.

Lunsford, Terry F. (ed.). *The Study of Academic Administration.* Boulder, Colo.: Western Interstate Commission for Higher Education, 1963.

MacIver, Robert M. *Academic Freedom in Our Time.* New York: Columbia University Press, 1955.

McVey, Frank L., and Raymond M. Hughes. *Problems of College and University Administration.* Ames, Iowa: The Iowa State College Press, 1952.

Millett, John D. *The Academic Community: An Essay on Organization.* New York: McGraw-Hill Book Company, Inc., 1962.

Presthus, Robert. *The Organizational Society.* New York: Alfred A. Knopf, 1962.

––––––. "University Bosses: The Executive Conquest of Academe," *The New Republic,* Vol. 152 (February 20, 1965).

Rourke, Francis E., and Glenn E. Brooks. *The Managerial Revolution in Higher Education.* Baltimore: The Johns Hopkins Press, 1966.

Rudolph, Frederick. *The American College and University.* New York: Alfred A. Knopf, 1962.

Williams, George. *Some of My Best Friends Are Professors.* New York: Abelard-Schuman, 1958.

Wilson, Logan. *The Academic Man.* New York: Oxford University Press, 1942.

AMERICAN COUNCIL ON EDUCATION

Logan Wilson, *President* .

The American Council on Education, founded in 1918, is a *council* of educational organizations and institutions. Its purpose is to advance education and educational methods through comprehensive voluntary and cooperative action on the part of American educational associations, organizations, and institutions.